TEACHING IS
INTERACTION

TEACHING IS
INTERACTION

A PRIMER OF IDEAS FOR TEACHERS

Dr. Richard H. Powell

XULON PRESS

Xulon Press
2301 Lucien Way #415
Maitland, FL 32751
407.339.4217
www.xulonpress.com

© 2023 by Dr. Richard H. Powell

All rights reserved solely by the author. The author guarantees all contents are original and do not infringe upon the legal rights of any other person or work. No part of this book may be reproduced in any form without the permission of the author.

Due to the changing nature of the Internet, if there are any web addresses, links, or URLs included in this manuscript, these may have been altered and may no longer be accessible. The views and opinions shared in this book belong solely to the author and do not necessarily reflect those of the publisher. The publisher therefore disclaims responsibility for the views or opinions expressed within the work.

Unless otherwise indicated, Scripture quotations taken from the New King James Version (NKJV). Copyright © 1982 by Thomas Nelson, Inc. Used by permission. All rights reserved.

Paperback ISBN-13: 978-1-66287-771-1
Ebook ISBN-13: 978-1-66287-772-8

Table of Contents

INTRODUCTION TO TEACHING vii

PART ONE: DECLINING VALUES IN EDUCATION 9

Chapter 1: Background American History 11
Chapter 2: Worldviews and Christian Education 15

PART TWO: INSTRUCTIONAL PLANNING AND TEACHING SKILLS 21

Introduction 23
Chapter 3: Curriculum Selection 25
Chapter 4: Writing Goals and Objectives 27
Chapter 5: Methods and Strategies of Instruction 35

PART THREE: FACTORS THAT INFLUENCE LEARNING 41

Introduction 43
Chapter 6: Learning Theory 45
Chapter 7: Types of Intelligence 49
Chapter 8: Learning Styles 55
Chapter 9: Teacher Effectiveness 63

PART FOUR: IDEAS FOR EVALUATION 71

Introduction 73

Bibliography 77

Introduction to Teaching

IF YOU GREW up in most American communities in the early or mid-twentieth century, your experience in public schools was vastly different than what is happening in today's schools.

Most schools took two days in November to celebrate Thanksgiving. December was filled with Christmas programs and carol singing at school, and schools were given two weeks to celebrate the true meaning of Christmas, along with enjoying the mystical "Santa Clause," who gives gifts. During the spring, another school break was given to recognize the significance of Good Friday and Easter.

Today's public schools can no longer recognize the true meaning of these dates that are important to Christian families. School breaks are now "winter" or "spring" breaks, and all of the above Christian events and references to God's love and Providence are being removed from public buildings, places, and public schools. Religious practices and events that were once the basic "educational foundations" of early American communities and schools are being removed also.

Worldviews have grown rapidly and are transforming public schools into government-controlled institutions, and they are trying to take over the primary role of parents and replace Judeo-Christian values with secular views. Parents and churches need to return to the values established by the Founding Fathers in the Declaration of Independence, the U.S. Constitution, and the Northwest Ordinance.

It seems that government domination of schools is a rebellion against Christian education.[1] It is a fact that secular education and Christian education have mutually exclusive goals and purposes, and according to Stephen C. Perks, "An education that denies God and His Word ... is an education that implicitly denies the whole of biblical truth and the validity of the Christian faith."[2]

The purpose of this book is to help teachers teach more effectively and to provide educational ideas that are helpful. These ideas will be reminders of things teachers already know and will improve teachers' skills in ways that will impact student academic and spiritual growth. Most of these educational ideas come from many authors and books listed in the bibliography.

The "Art of Teaching"

The following ideas come from many sources, and some are ideas that I have learned during my fifty years in the field of education. Teaching is a "skillful art" that results in positive learning outcomes for the "student." The teacher's interaction with students is the key to successful student learning.

I am assuming that teachers and/or instructors of different subjects, such as science or the social sciences, will be more effective if they use the interactive skills presented in this booklet, as teaching is an interactive process.

The key to the effective teaching/learning process is the teacher, who controls most of the variables within the instructional environment and the curriculum materials.

This booklet is a primer of ideas, methods, and skills that will help the teacher help the learner have a successful learning experience. Once again, teaching is interaction, and the teacher is the key.

---

[1] Douglas Wilson, *The Case for Classical Christian Education*, Wheaton, IL: Crossway Books, 2003, 55.

[2] Ibid., 54.

Part One: Declining Values In Education

Chapter I:

Background American History

Since the beginning of history, disobeying God's commands has always resulted in moral and spiritual consequences for the individual, a family, and a nation.

In a recent book, George Barna stated that "America was approaching an era of moral and ritual anarchy."[1] Barna believes that in time, people will not be affected by laws, church teachings, or family values. They will do whatever they want, regardless of prevailing mores in society.

Dr. Richard Land, another authority on Christian ethics, said, "America is facing one of the deepest moral and spiritual crises in her history, the degeneration of the American family." [2] Both Barna and Land believe that the solution to the moral, spiritual crisis will depend on Christian leaders and families. [3]

For many years, Christian authorities have recognized that secularism in our schools and society is a primary cause for moral degeneration in the American family and nation. Many American parents have assumed that public schools are teaching traditional Judeo-Christian moral values along with academic subjects. But within the last fifty years, many of our

---

[1] George Barna, *A Fish Out of Water,* Nashville: Integrity Publishers, 2002, xxv.

[2] Richard Land & John Perry, *Real Homeland Security: How Godly Parents Protect a Nation*. Colorado: Alive Communications Inc., 2003, ix.

[3] Ibid., p. ix.

"traditional" moral and spiritual values that were once a vital part of our American schooling have been gradually removed from public schools and society.

Therefore, as America's moral and spiritual roots decline, Christian parents and churches need to challenge this degeneration by supporting Christian school education.

Several years ago, Paul Harvey said this: "For a hundred years the Protestant church and public education in the United States were intertwined and, most of us assumed, inseparable." [4] However, a brief review of America's early schools will show how education changed from its religious and biblical emphasis to the current non-religious purposes.

The two main institutions ordained by God for raising and educating children were the "family" and the "church."[5]

Early American grammar schools had religious purposes and an emphasis on moral values. The education of those who settled "America was uniquely Christian and Bible-based."[6]

When children in the colonial period learned their ABCs, they also learned Bible doctrine and Bible stories from the New England Primer and McGuffey Reader.[7]

In higher education, a moral and religious emphasis was promoted by Christian leaders who founded nearly all the universities. Harvard, Yale, Columbia, Princeton, and many others had a heavy focus on training ministers to preach and teach the Bible. Dr. D. James Kennedy states that "Almost every one of the first 123 colleges and universities in the United States has Christian origins."[8]

---

[4] Paul Harvey, forward to *The Christian School: Why It is Right for your Child*. Victor Books, 1974, 7.

[5] Land, Op. cit., 1.

[6] David C. Gibbs and Jerry Newcombe, *One Nation Under God*, Florida: Christian Law Association, 2005, 65.

[7] Ibid., 66.

[8] Ibid,. 74.

Background American History

Biblical principles and governmental politics were compatible in America's early history. For example, in 1789, the First Amendment to the Bill of Rights was freedom of religion. An important provision to the Northwest Ordinance said, "Religion, morality, and knowledge being necessary to good government and the happiness of mankind, schools and the means of education shall forever be encouraged."[9] Today, public schools and society are becoming "religion free zones."[10]

In the past one hundred years, our biblical roots have been gradually removed from public education, resulting in moral degeneration. Early in the 20th century, Horace Mann, Charles Darwin, and John Dewey had a profound influence in changing the biblical moral teachings in education. Horace Mann, called the "Father of public schools" in America, along with Thomas Dewey's "progressive education," were part of the larger movement known as secular humanism. This secular movement rejected the biblical beliefs of God's statutes of morality and focused on man's ability to discover truth and solve life's problems without supernatural help. No doubt, these "educational reformers" and leaders were borrowing ideas from past history, such as ancient Greek teachers like Plato and Socrates, who believed that man could discover wisdom and truth through philosophy.

In the mid-twentieth century, humanists were declaring that "the ultimate source of truth ... is found in science and nature."[11] And these "intellectuals" were rejecting the words in Proverbs 1-2 that declare that truth and wisdom do not come from man's intellect and philosophy, but God reveals and gives all wisdom and truth to man.

In 1949, T. S. Eliot warned that threats to Judeo-Christian values were coming from a pagan and humanistic culture.[12] And in the late 1970s, Dr. David L. Hocking provided the following warnings and trends in public education: 1) The removal of the Bible from public schools and society and

---

[9] Ibid., 69.

[10] Ibid., 79.

[11] Land, Op. cit., 12.

[12] Ibid.

2) God's Word being replaced with man presuming to have the ability to discover "truth" through science.[13]

It is apparent that these trends are accelerating today, and the removal of biblical and moral teachings from public schools has kept many public-school students from hearing and learning that man's sin nature is the primary cause of America's moral degeneration.

---

[13] David L. Hocking , The Theological Basis for the Philosophy of Christian School Education," *The Philosophy of Christian School Education*. ASCI, 1978, (Paul A. Kienel, editor of 3rd ed.), 8-12.

Chapter 2:

Worldviews and Christian Education

MANY YEARS AGO, Martin Luther wrote this prophetic warning: "I am much afraid that the Universities and schools will prove to be the gates of hell, unless they diligently labor explaining the Holy Scripture. I advise no one to place his child where the Scriptures do not reign paramount."[14]

Critics of Christian education have argued that Christian schools segregate children from society[15] and the "real world."[16] But parents need to protect and shelter their children until they can withstand the influences found at many of today's schools and colleges, which try to keep young people from a Christian worldview.[17]

Although positive accomplishments have come from public schools and colleges over the years, many of the positive outcomes can be attributed to dedicated Christian teachers who have spent their life and whole career teaching in public schools. Nevertheless, the major issue in society and public education is what Dr. James Dobson calls the "civil war of values." Dobson is referring to Judeo-Christian values, which today can only be taught in a Christian school environment and by Christian teachers who

---

[14] Gibbs, Op. cit., 68.

[15] Paul A. Kienel, *The Christian School: Why It is Right for Your Child*. 1974, 23.

[16] Henry Morris, *Education for the Real World*. Creation Life Publishers, 1977, 7.

[17] Kienel, Op. cit. 54.

may freely teach the Scriptures and promote moral and spiritual values and integrate them throughout the curriculum.

Worldviews Today

There are many philosophies and worldviews about the origin of life and the universe. But the two primary worldviews that have had the greatest impact in American culture and education during the past two centuries are the biblical Judeo-Christian view and the secular-humanist view.

The Biblical Worldview. The biblical view says 1) God is Creator of all things, 2) man was created in God's image, 3) Adam's disobedience resulted in sin and death being passed to all human generations, and 4) salvation comes from the Lord, and it is given to those whom the Lord chooses (Ps. 3:8).[18]

The main problem in public school education is that the people who have been elected to serve on school boards over the past two or three decades have been rejecting the view of God's revelation of creation and truth about the origin of life and the universe and have accepted secular-humanism's view and the theory of evolution as being "true science." This humanistic view assumes that science and man's intellect can explain and/or uncover the origins of life and the universe.

The biblical Judeo-Christian view of early American culture and the history of government and public education focused on God's Word as truth regarding creation of life and the universe.

The Bible clearly teaches intelligent design, and for Christian educators, the Master Designer is Jesus Christ, Who **"In the beginning was the Word ... and the Word was God ... and the Word became flesh" (John 1).**

---

[18] Eugene H. Birdsall, "How to Implement the Christian Philosophy," *v*, ASCI, 1978, (Paul A. Kienel, Editor of 3rd edition), 47.

Secular Humanism

The secular-humanist view says: 1) There is no God, 2) all things in the universe are the result of an evolutionary process, 3) man is basically good, and bad behavior is caused by factors in the political and social environment, and 4) man can learn and know all things without supernatural involvement.[19]

All of these views must be challenged and rejected by Christians because public school students are being brainwashed with self-concept and self-actualization psychology and philosophy that came into vogue beginning in the 1960s. The main idea of perceptual psychology is that man is basically good.[20]

Abraham Maslow's hierarchy of needs states that man can reach the pinnacle of success through the process of healthy growth and the gratification of basic needs. This can be accomplished because man's nature is basically good and not evil.* Even the most recent history provides evidence that men like Hitler, Osama bin Laden, and Islamic terrorists demonstrate the biblical truth that men have an inborn sin nature that is evil, and these unregenerate men demonstrate their evil nature.

In past history, both of the above views have been in a "cosmic and earthly battle" because of man's sin nature. Today, the historical religious worldview from the sixth and seventh centuries is returning once again under the false religious view of radical Islam. The Bible has always warned of false religious philosophies and pagan gods. Satan is called an "angel of light," who is a deceiver to all mankind.

Jesus warned us about Satan and his false prophets, who come to us in **"sheep's clothing, but inwardly they are ravenous wolves" (Matt. 7:15).**

These opposing worldviews identify the historical conflict between God's way and man's way. But the Lord identifies and also explains the age-old

---

[19] Ibid.

[20] David Delk, "Theology for Ordinary Life," *By Faith*, (magazine), Published by the Presbyterian Church in America, May-June, 2005, 25-27.

conflict in His own words: **"For my thoughts are not your thoughts, nor are your ways My ways" declares the Lord. For as the heavens are higher than the earth, so are My ways higher than your ways, and My thoughts than your thoughts" (Isa. 55:8-9).** Yet, man thinks that through his intellect and science, he is able to arrive at truth and unlock the mysteries of life in the universe.

A Christian Philosophy of Education

The best way for Christian parents to challenge the degeneration of moral and spiritual values is to lead their children to believe in Jesus for salvation and teach their children to walk daily in the ways of the Lord (Deut. 6:5-9).

The next step is to provide their children with a Christian school education that teaches a biblical worldview and reinforces the parent's belief that Jesus Christ is the only way to receive the gift of eternal life. Below are a few essential teachings of a Christian school philosophy of education:

1. A Christian philosophy recognizes God as Creator and source of truth and acknowledges that Jesus Christ is the God-Man and the only way of eternal life in heaven.
2. Administrative leaders must put Christ first in their lives and demonstrate that commitment before students and staff.
3. Teachers and staff must have a personal relationship with the Lord and an excellent knowledge of the Bible.
4. A Christian philosophy of education focuses on the student's spiritual relationship with the Lord and academic growth.
5. The Bible is the foundation and central core of the curriculum.[21]
6. The purpose of a Christian education is to help students recognize their sin nature, understand their need to receive Christ, and strengthen their faith in Christ.

Summary

The primary responsibility of God's plan for the education of children has been given to parents. During America's early history, educational purposes were based on biblical principles, teachings, and freedoms that were incorporated in the Declaration of Independence and the United States Constitution.

During the nineteenth and twentieth centuries, educational purposes were changing from an emphasis on Judeo-Christian teachings to secular-humanist ideas in education, which began to dominate teaching in the social and physical sciences in schools and universities.

These changes from biblical worldviews to secular views have resulted in the rejection of moral and spiritual values and laws and the prevention of biblical symbols from being displayed in public places, buildings, and schools, all of which has contributed to America's moral decay in family life and the American culture.

Parents and churches must work together to support Christian schools and to continue to play a vital role in helping children and young people strengthen their knowledge and faith in God's plan for their life.

Part Two: Instructional Planning and Teaching Skills

Introduction

THE FOUNDATION OF American education was presented in Part One. The purpose of this section is to provide some suggestions for teachers and educators in public or private schools for instructional planning and teaching skills.

The first phase of a paradigm or model for establishing an educational program involves describing the theological and/or philosophical foundation for the educational program. God's Word is the central focus of Christian education, and usually, the church has the primary responsibility in that phase.[1]

Part Two is the second phase of the preparation to implement the educational program and will require support from the church and supporters of Christian education. The focus in this section will be to offer some ideas of their teaching skills and methods that will improve the quality of education. There are many areas that can be studied, but some of the critical areas are as follows: 1) Selecting curricula that fits the philosophy of education for the school, 2) writing goals and objectives, 3) identifying appropriate teaching methods and strategies, 4) identifying the abilities of students in the school and community being served, 5) evaluating teacher effectiveness, 6) monitoring and evaluating the instructional program, and 7) working with the church, school board, parents, and community.

The areas listed above represent many of the tasks that teachers and administrators deal with on a daily basis. However, hiring quality teachers and administrators who agree with the educational philosophy and curriculum is the most critical part of educational programs.

---

[1] Eugene H. Birdsall, "How to Implement the Christian Philosophy," *The Philosophy of Christian School Education*. ASCI, 1978, (Paul A. Kienel, Editor, 3rd Edition, p.54.

Chapter 3:

Curriculum Selection

Selecting a curriculum that will fit into the overall philosophy and mission is one of the more difficult tasks facing Christian educators because there are so many worldview philosophies, books, and materials from which to choose. The selection task should be a cooperative effort that involves pastors, administrators, teachers, curriculum specialists, and parents.

All educational programs and curriculum materials that have been used for several years should be regularly examined, and those that have been tried and proven effective should continue to be used and evaluated.

Curriculum development is an ongoing process and an important part of maintaining quality education. Systematic program evaluation is an essential aspect for monitoring and assessing the many variables involved in the educational program.

Chapter 4:

Writing Goals and Objectives

Once the curriculum has been determined, writing goals and objectives related to the curriculum content begins. Goals and objectives identify the important academic outcomes and the moral and spiritual values that students will need in their future.

This is a difficult task for teachers because of the need to make sure that the goals and objectives are tied to the curriculum, the teaching methods, and the program evaluation. Very often, educators and teachers quickly write vague goals and objectives without clearly identifying the subject matter and how to evaluate the degree of success or failure to meet the goals and objectives. Below are a few examples of some goal statements that illustrate how vague a goal statement can be:

School District Goals:

1. Each student should develop a sense of self-worth.
2. Each student should acquire attitudes, knowledge, and habits that will permit him/her to function effectively as a responsible citizen.

A Teacher's Classroom Goals:

1. Teach students the basic rules of civilized behavior.
2. Nourish the social and creative lives of each student.

You can see that these statements are vague and open to many interpretations regarding the subject matter, teaching methods, and how to evaluate them.

Here is another example: "My goal is to teach kids to be creative and responsible thinkers of society." This sounds good, but the problem with this and all of the above examples is that these statements need to be more clearly and specifically defined. What content will be used in teaching?

What method will be used? How will the teacher determine if the goal(s) has been reached? This is the purpose of writing objectives.

A Procedure for Writing Goals and Objectives

Below is a brief step-by-step process for writing goals and objectives which will provide ways to evaluate teaching and instruction:

1. Define the educational philosophy.
2. Select the curriculum/content to be taught.
3. Write goals and objectives related to the content you plan to evaluate.
4. Determine teaching methods that fit the content, goals, and objectives.
5. Evaluate the instructional outcomes.

Robert Miller[2] offers excellent advice on the role of philosophy in selecting curriculum materials and writing goals and objectives. Once the philosophy and curriculum have been determined, a helpful step is to make a brief outline of the essential concepts in the curricula materials and/or subjects that the teacher(s) plans to teach. Some published textbooks and materials organize subject matter into units or chapters, which can be helpful when preparing an outline that identifies the "broad" concepts.

---

[2] Robert Miller, "Implementing the Christian Philosophy in Textbook Selection and General Curriculum Development," *The Philosophy of Christian School Education*. ASCI, 1978, (Paul A. Kienel, Editor, 3rd Edition, Chapter six.

Writing Goals and Objectives

This can be helpful when trying to zero in on the broad areas of a subject to be taught/learned.

In addition, some of the books and materials have included goals and objectives for the teacher to consider. Some curriculum materials provide some goals and objectives, but the teacher may have to revise them or develop their own goals and objectives for the content to fit their own methods.

One textbook used in some educational programs is called *Teaching in the Middle and Secondary Schools,* by Joseph Callahan, et. al. Module Three explains the purpose for preparing an
  outline of your subject matter and how a brief outline can be used in writing goals and objectives.[3]

Writing Goals

As suggested, develop a brief outline of the content you plan to teach. It will help identify the subject matter for writing goals. Each goal statement should identify at least two essential elements. For example, a goal should identify 1) a broad subject, such as government, algebra, or science, and 2) the type of student learning behavior, such as "cognitive" knowledge of the subject to be learned. You could write the goal as an "affective behavior," such as, "The student exhibits an <u>interest</u> in government or algebra."

Below is one example of a broad (knowledge) goal for the subject of American government:

1. **"Students in American <u>government</u> will demonstrate a <u>knowledge</u> of government."**

As you can see, this goal is very broad, and the subject matter will need to be divided into smaller facts and topics of government, such as voting,

---

[3] Joseph F. Callahan, et, al., *Teaching in the Middle and Secondary Schools.* 7th Edition, 2002.

citizenship, Congress, branches of government, the Constitution, democracy, etc.

An example of a broad affective (interest) goal statement for American government could be something like the following example: "**Students in American <u>government</u> will demonstrate an <u>interest</u> in government.**"

The main point is that a broad goal of a certain subject needs to have many smaller, specific objectives related to the subject content to be learned.

<u>Writing Objectives</u>

Writing specific objectives related to the goal is the next step in the process. The goal statement is very broad; the objective is more specific. Objectives are written with enough clarity that will help the teacher and student recognize what, when, and how the objective is to be evaluated. Therefore, objectives need to identify elements that will help in the assessment process or testing.

Numerous objectives can be developed from a single goal statement. Objectives break down the subject matter into smaller topics of subject matter and more specific facts students are learning. Objectives "more specifically identify" things like the student's knowledge of subject matter (content) and how the objective will be assessed or evaluated.

For example, the basic parts of an objective can identify the 1) age/grade of the student(s), 2) the specific subject/content, 3) the student's specific cognitive and/or affective behavior, and 4) when and/or how to measure (evaluate) the outcome to determine the degree to which the objective was met. That is the role of the test.

Below is an example of a specific objective in algebra:

1. At end of the unit, students will demonstrate comprehension and application of the following Algebra I concepts, as measured by the department criterion test.

- Simplify expressions using distributive property and combining like terms.
- Find absolute value of a number.
- Graph numbers on a number line.
- Solve equations with variable terms on each side.

The main point is to identify the content to be taught by the teacher and learned by the student.

In the textbook by Callahan, et.al., Module Three does a good job of explaining the importance of goals and objectives. Modules Nine and Ten deal with assessment.

A Common Format and Terminology

This brings up another helpful aspect of writing goals and objectives. Teachers and educators should agree on using a common format and common terminology for understanding goals, objectives, and evaluation within the same school or district.

This approach will greatly improve common communication and understanding of the process and will help all instructional staff be on the same page when discussing these instructional objectives, terms, definitions, and how they will be evaluated across the curriculum.

One example might be to use *Bloom's Taxonomy of Educational Objectives*[4] to define behavioral terms. This would mean that all teachers would be using the same behavioral terms when writing goals and objectives.

Bloom's Taxonomy provides definitions and a hierarchy of behavioral terms from simple to complex levels of cognitive behaviors, such as knowledge, comprehension, application, analysis, synthesis, and evaluation. This approach will improve the understanding of desired outcomes for the

---

[4] Benjamin S. Boom, Editor, *Taxonomy of Educational Objectives*. N.Y.: David McKay, Inc. 1956.

objectives to be evaluated. There is also an effective taxonomy of behavioral terms to deal with attitude, interest, and value type behaviors.

Let me offer the following analogy as the reason for having one format or one set of definitions. It seems reasonable to me for a school to have one set of policies for all teachers to use when handling classroom discipline, rather than letting all teachers handle school discipline matters in their own individual way.

If every teacher applied their own rules to discipline, students would play all kinds of games with teachers, parents, and administrators. Chaos would surely result from this kind of environment. Therefore, common rules and policies will prevent the potential chaos that would result if teachers did their own thing in the school.

The Teacher and School Approach to Goals and Objectives

Goals and objectives in a Christian school will have different purposes, especially when it comes to teachings of moral and spiritual values. But the purpose for writing goals and objectives is to clearly state what the student is to learn.

Gene Garrick[5] and Eugene Birdsall[6] present a Christian perspective on goals and objectives that encourages teachers to focus on 1) academic achievement, 2) spiritual and moral growth, 3) personal and social development, and 4) encourages parents to be actively involved in their child's education.

Cognitive and Affective Outcomes

Objectives that measure cognitive outcomes in math or science that normally have a right or wrong answer are usually easy to measure and score.

---

[5] Gene Garrick, "Developing Educational Objectives," *The Philosophy of Christian School Education*. ASCI, 1978, Paul A. Kienel, Editor, 3rd Edition.

[6] Birdsall, Op.Cit. 63.

Writing Goals and Objectives

But some cognitive objectives in history are also affective objectives that deal with character traits, integrity, responsibility, and moral and spiritual values and are much more difficult to <u>measure</u> and <u>score</u>, especially if there is no standard of "right or wrong" or truth. Of course, there is a biblical standard for Christians schools.

But, according to Arthur Combs, one of the basic principles of perceptual psychology is that "all behavior has affective qualities."[7] His opinion is that all behavior has some feeling or emotion that depends on personal meaning. Arthur Combs further states that "Learning is the discovery of personal meaning,"[8] and that the affective cannot be separated from the cognitive domain. "The fact is, unless education is affective there will be no learning at all."[9]

Some cognitive and affective behaviors seem to be inseparable. Thus, intellectual and emotional behaviors should come together when dealing with ethics and truth—that is God's truth. These are important points about affective behavior because all education seems to focus on values, morality, and spiritual outcomes that for some are more important than academic outcomes.

The point is that all education has a biblical "standard" for ethics and moral values, which is revealed in God's revelation of truth.

Summary Points for Writing Goals & Objectives

Writing clear goals and objectives helps teachers and students understand what is being taught and learned, and it will make a significant difference when it comes time to test and evaluate the instructional outcomes. Here are some brief steps to follow:

1. A philosophy of education is the foundation.

---

[7] A. W. Combs, *Myths In Education.* Boston: Allyn & Bacon, Inc. 1979, 162.

[8] Ibid. 161.

[9] Ibid. 162.

2. Selecting the curriculum content is a major part of instruction.
3. Write goals and objectives to identify outcomes of instruction.
4. Select methods that fit the goals/objectives and curriculum.
5. Evaluate to provide feedback for students, teachers, administration, parents, and the school board.

Chapter 5:

Methods and Strategies of Instruction

ONE OF THE instructional areas that is often overlooked by new teachers is the matter of teaching methods or strategies. One reason this happens is because some teachers assume that if *they* have mastered the content they teach, student learning will automatically happen. This is a mistake. Methods play a significant role in teaching.

In early American history, traditional Judeo-Christian values had a major influence on the culture and educational institutions. During the nineteenth and twentieth centuries in America, two opposing philosophies of education emerged: 1) Biblical creationism and 2) secular humanism. Because there were two opposing philosophies about human nature and culture, apparently some educators assumed there should be two different teaching methods or strategies in education, especially public schools.

James W. Braley[10] describes the two main teaching methods of instruction that have been used in education during the past two centuries as the "pouring-in" approach and the "drawing-out" approach.

---

[10] James W. Braley, "The Christian Philosophy Applied to Methods of Instruction," *The Philosophy of Christian School Education*, ASCI. 1978, (Paul A. Kienel, Editior, 3rd Edition, 96.

Pouring-in Approach/Method

The "pouring-in" approach/method stressed the need to acquire basic knowledge by filling up the student's mind with facts and memorized information. The teacher's task was to lecture and give information for students to memorize and be able to write or recite for the teacher. It was believed that the mind was like an "open container," and the teacher's role was to drill and pour information into the student's mind.

The Drawing-out Approach/Method

During the early 1900s, the "drawing-out" approach/method became popular. In this approach, the teacher focused less on accumulating facts and placed more emphasis on discovery, individualized learning, and establishing an environment that encouraged positive student attitudes and feelings. Thomas Dewey's "progressive education" movement in America promoted these ideas.

Methods and Beliefs

It should be noted that teaching methods are different from a person's religious or secular beliefs. For example, creationism and secular humanism mentioned above are a person's philosophical beliefs, attitudes, values, and purposes of life. Teaching methods and/or strategies primarily focus on different ways that students learn. Therefore, in a pedagogical or educational framework of teaching skills and techniques, student learning is more directly related to how students learn and not related directly to the learning of religious beliefs.[11]

Teaching methods are usually related to or refer to educational theories of learning, such as reinforcement, motivation, retention, how fast students learn, and the ability levels of students. Methods focus on such things as <u>how</u>

---

[11] Ibid. 113.

students learn and/or their <u>ability</u> to learn, not what religious or secular beliefs they are learning. Therefore, teachers should understand the difference between methods and beliefs.

The use of methods in teaching is very important because it is the teacher in the classroom who chooses the types of methods that will be used for the different types of learning. It is the teacher who helps or hinders learning achievement and primarily controls the interpersonal relationships that develop between the teacher and the student.[12] Additional information about motivational relationships resulting from teacher and student interactions in the classroom will be further discussed in Part Three of this book.

Contemporary Methods

Two contemporary groups of methods used widely today in education/schools are defined and explained in greater detail in the previously cited textbook by Joseph Callahan, et.al. One of the modules in the Callahan textbook describes a group of methods called **teacher-centered strategies**.[13]

This group of methods is called "teacher-centered strategies" because they focus on teacher strategies that use lecture, demonstration, question and answer, drills, and memorization of information. These are very much like the traditional methods of the "pouring-in" approach used in America's early educational approach.

The second group of methods, called **student-centered strategies**,[14] utilizes such strategies and techniques as inquiry and discovery learning, cooperative learning, individualized projects, and self-learning activities. The focus of student-centered strategies is to involve the individual students in their own learning, while the teacher's task is to act as a facilitator of student learning, rather than a dispenser of knowledge. Here, too, you

---

[12] Ibid. 116.

[13] Callahan, Op. Cit. 251.

[14] Ibid. 209.

can see a likeness to the "drawing-out" approach that received emphasis in the early 1900s.

It should also be noted that both of these methods/strategies are widely used today in American public and private education. The pendulum swings slowly in education, and it's difficult to know if one approach is best. In reality, both approaches are appropriate and valid.

The Bible and Teaching Methods

Currently, both groups of strategies mentioned above are currently used in public and religious schools, and it should be no surprise to Christian educators to realize that both of these groups of strategies and/or methods are biblically based.

James Braley provides a list of biblical examples that demonstrates that both of these groups of methods are widely used throughout the Bible.[15] Although biblical and secular beliefs are very different, we should remember that methods deal with *how*, not *what* students learn.

But the most important truth about teaching methods is that the Bible uses all of these methods. Teaching methods originated with God, and they have been demonstrated by God's servants for generations. All kinds of methods were beautifully demonstrated by Jesus, the Master Teacher, Who taught and demonstrated through parables, lectures, examples, and discovery, all of the methods which have become teaching models for Christian teachers to use for teaching "doctrine, for reproof, for correction, for instruction in righteousness that the man of God may be complete, thoroughly equipped for every good work" (2 Tim. 3:16).

Classical Christian Education and Methods

Teaching methods can be defined in different ways, and there are numerous terms used to describe the techniques that a teacher might use to

---

[15] Braley, Op. Cit. 104.

motivate and help a student learn more effectively. Classical Christian educators offer their approach as another way of defining and thinking about teaching methods.

The classical education approach to teaching subjects in a curriculum is defined by two groups of subjects. One group is called the trivium, which includes the subjects of grammar, logic, and rhetoric. The second group of subjects is called the quadrivium, which includes geometry, astronomy, music, and arithmetic.

Through the study of these subjects, the students (K-12) will learn God's truth and wisdom. Classical teachers and educators believe that students who graduate from a classical education program will be prepared for any career, whether it is in science, law, medicine, business, or ministry.[16]

According to a well-known classical educator, Dorothy Sayers, "The trivium subjects are not really subjects at all but the means or method for handling and learning subjects—a kind of master art (tool) that enables one to study any subject."[17] It is often assumed and believed by many educators that students learn subject matter without actually learning how to learn. Therefore, classical educators believe that the trivium subjects are the basic methods and tools of learning that teach students how to learn for themselves.[18]

Most Christian educators will agree that teaching God's Word is the primary goal of education, and a classical education offers a system of methods or "tools" for students to learn and receive God's wisdom and truth.

The classical approach emphasizes that there are three developmental stages of learning. For example, grammar (factual information) is taught at the K-6 level, logic (debate and discussion) at the 7-9 level, and rhetoric (persuasive speaking and writing) at the high school level.[19]

---

[16] Christopher A. Perrin, *An Introduction to Classical Education: A Guide for Parents*, Harrisburg, PA: Classical Academic Press. 2004, 31.

[17] Ibid., 20.

[18] Ibid., 29.

[19] Ibid., 22.

Variables That Influence Methods and Learning

Methods are very important to the teaching-learning process and can help or hinder learning and impact learning and/or achievement. There are many variables in teaching that influence instructional effectiveness and new teachers. Below is a brief list of important variables related to effective teaching:

1) Teacher skills
2) Grade level content
3) Student ability
4) Student modalities and learning styles
5) Materials, equipment, and facilities
6) Time of day and time for instruction
7) The classroom environment

These and other variables will be discussed in Part Three.

Part Three: Factors That Influence – Learning

Introduction

During the past decades, learning has been defined by some, such as Piaget, Maslow, and others, as a kind of developmental process or change. In order to avoid some confusion,

Morris Bigge distinguishes between the terms "learning" and "maturation" by pointing out that maturation is a physical developmental process, while learning is an intellectual change in a person's insight, behavior, perception, motivation, or a combination of these.[1] Assuming this is a valid distinction, it would seem that teachers can do little about a student's maturation, but they can have a significant impact on a student's learning. The information and discussion that follows will focus on the role of the teacher and factors that influence learning in the school classroom environment.

Most, if not all, teachers have experienced teaching a lesson with a mixed response from the students. For example, some kids seem to learn and understand the lesson material quickly, while others have a blank look on their face and don't seem to have a clue as to what you are trying to teach. I'm quite sure that most teachers have experienced some aspects of that kind of classroom scenario and asked the following question: "Why is it that when I teach a lesson, some kids get it quickly, while others just don't get it?" While the response from some students is a clear understanding of the lesson, the response of others is the "blank" look or a "who cares" look.

At this point, the teacher may follow up his/her questions by saying to the class, "I just covered that information. I gave you the answers and

---

[1] Morris L. Bigge, *Learning Theories for Teachers*, N.Y: Harper & Row, 1964, 1.

explained everything! Why don't you listen to me, and why can't you remember it?"

Usually, when this kind of event happens in a classroom, a teacher may begin to rationalize or defend their teaching by saying to themselves, "I think some students just hate school and they are deliberately trying not to listen to what I'm trying to teach them.

I'm sure many teachers have experienced episodes like this and had some of these thoughts about students. But did you stop to think that the lack of a student's understanding might be related to your teaching skills, rather than a problem with the students?

For example, it could be that some students just needed to hear the lesson explained again in a different way or demonstrated visually, along with the lecture explanation. It is possible that you didn't make it clear the first time, even though it was perfectly clear and understandable to you. It could be that the information you were teaching wasn't perceived by some students as having any personal meaning, or it wasn't exciting or motivating.

Maybe some of those students couldn't see any immediate purpose for them at that moment in time, and maybe some students didn't have previous experiences to draw upon to understand the lesson material.

Understanding why some learn fast and others learn more slowly is part of a student's ability, previous experience, and the teaching-learning process. This is a real challenge for teachers, and the scenario above is a typical experience for many students and teachers.

Therefore, the following information in Part Three will examine some of the reasons why this happens and will suggest ways that will help both the students and the teachers deal with these classroom situations. Chapters six, seven, eight, and nine will discuss these areas.

Chapter 6:

Learning Theory and Ideas

Theories of learning make assumptions concerning the basic nature of man. I will only mention a few historical examples. The Socratic method seemed to imply that students already had a certain amount of intellectual knowledge within themselves, and therefore, it was the role of the teacher to draw it out through the skillful process of questioning. This method, used by the ancient Greek philosopher Socrates, implied that the teacher didn't have complete knowledge but did have the skill to "draw" knowledge out of the student.

During the early part of modern history, Rousseau, Darwin, and other evolutionists theorized that man was merely a higher form of animal; therefore, learning for humans was similar to that of animals.[2]

By the early part of the twentieth century, basically two families of "learning theory" emerged from Darwinian assumptions: 1) Behaviorism, and 2) Gestalt-field psychology.

Using rats in their research, the behaviorists stated that the "results of animal experimentation is governed by the assumptions that the learning process is essentially the same throughout the animal kingdom and what we discover about animal learning is transferable to human situations."[3] This was the same assumption made by Rousseau.[4] The work of Pavlov and

---

[2] Ibid., 87.

[3] Ibid., 86.

[4] Ibid., 87.

Thorndike made the same assumptions, which were widely held opinions of behaviorists until the Gestalt-field theorists challenged the behaviorists' theory with the position that "learning always involves purpose."[5] The Gestalt-field group began asking such questions as: "Do animals learn like men?"[6] "Do animals do things randomly or with a purpose in mind?" and "Why not use humans to study learning, rather than rats and dogs?"[7]

To the Gestalt psychologists, purpose and personal meaning were critical factors in learning. The behaviorists defined behavior as something that is visible and observable, while the Gestalt group defined behavior as a change in a person's personal perception or purpose that is not "directly observable."[8] By the mid-twentieth century, this new force in psychology emerged to add their views to behavior and learning. The 1962 ASCD Yearbook called *Perceiving, Behaving, Becoming*[9] reported viewpoints of this "third force" in psychology. A couple familiar names and works of these perceptual psychologists include Abraham Maslow's self-actualizing psychology and Arthur W. Combs's viewpoints on perception. One of the basic principles of perception states: "Behaving and learning are products of perceiving."[10] These perceptual psychologies state that self-concept and values are learned and perceptions come from experiences: "Since all of these ways of perceiving are learned, they can also be taught."[11] These psychologists added the "human" aspect of perception, purpose, and meaning to the previous "animal" theories of instinct and conditioning.

---

[5] Ibid., 89

[6] Ibid., 88.

[7] Ibid., 93.

[8] Ibid., 103.

[9] Abraham Maslow, "Some Basic Propositions of a Growth and Self-Actualizing Psychology," Perceiving, Behaving, Becoming, ASCD, Washington, D.C.:NEA, 1962, p. 1. 34.

[10] Arthur Combs, "Perceiving and Behaving," Perceiving, Behaving, Becoming, ASCD, Washington, D.C.: NEA, p.67.

[11] Ibid., 61.

A large body of the research mentioned above is related to the learning process that has been conducted during the past decade. These research studies have reported challenging information to the findings of behaviorism and the "third force" psychology.

While some of the ideas are helpful regarding the problem of understanding the learning process, there is a major misunderstanding about human nature. For Christians, these philosophies and psychologies from the mid-twentieth century make the following claims:

1) Man's inborn genetic nature is good, not evil, and 2) man is part of the evolutionary process of the animal kingdom. Thus, man is not created in God's image and likeness, nor does he have a spiritual or eternal soul. This is a major difference between modern worldview psychologies and philosophies and the biblical worldview of human nature.

Contemporary Influences of Learning

This section will discuss some additional studies that have identified factors that have significant implications on learning and teaching of students in public, private, and Christian schools. A brief review of some of these factors that influence learning are:

1. Intelligence quotients
2. Multiple intelligences
3. Emotional intelligence
4. Learning styles
5. Student-teacher interaction
6. Classroom climate

The issues related to intelligence are too numerous to be examined in a brief review of these topics. Therefore, intelligence will receive a limited discussion of some of the factors that influence teaching and learning in the school classroom.

For example, the controversial information on intelligence in *The Bell Curve* by Richard Hermstein and Charles Murray is not part of this focus. Also, only a few brief points of the research conducted by Bernice McCarthy, Rita and Kenneth Dunn, Anthony Gregoric, Howard Gardner, Daniel Goleman, Ned Flanders, and E. J. Amidon will be presented, as they relate to certain aspects of classroom teaching and learning. The textbook by Callahan, et al., is a resource for some of the topics in Part Three of this book.

But because the focus of this booklet is primarily addressed to Christian educators, the following two books are recommended: *The Way They Learn* by Cynthia Ulrich Tobias and *Learning Styles: Reaching Everyone God Gave You To Teach* by Marlene D. Le Fever.

Chapter 7:

Types of Intelligence

Recently, I saw a cartoon that pictured a young boy standing in front of his parents who were holding their son's report card filled with Ds.

The boy's comment to his parents was this: "It's not all my fault. I did the best I could with the genes you gave me." That answer may have some truth; however, current research has a lot of information to add to that traditional position.

The "intelligence quotient" has been around for many years, and it has traditionally been used to identify and predict the likelihood of a person's potential for achievement, occupational success, or performance in schools and society. IQ test scores show there are significant differences among a population of students and persons who take IQ tests. IQ scores have proven to be indictors of cognitive differences, primarily in verbal and mathematical abilities. However, IQ scores have also generated many controversial issues about intelligence, such as 1) whether intelligence is inherited or molded by environment, 2) how IQ scores are used and misused, and 3) what are the best ways to use IQ scores.

Contemporary Research Studies

The focus in this section will be to examine a few of the implications that intelligence may have on the teaching and learning process.

Barbara Clark's book *Optimizing Learning* reports some contemporary studies related to brain research that suggest that intelligence tests reflect only certain aspects of a person's competence, and therefore, we must rethink our beliefs about learning. Clark's Integrative Education Model focuses on a system that involves learner's thoughts, feelings, senses, and intuition.[12] It is obvious that teachers need to look at different factors that influence learning, and many educators, such as Callahan et al., have agreed that the educational implications regarding intelligence indicate that 1) intelligence is not fixed, but can be learned or developed, and 2) not all students learn in the same way.[13]

Multiple Intelligences

Traditional IQ testing mainly emphasized verbal and mathematical measures, but the research of Howard Gardner suggests that there are seven types of intelligence.[14]

For example, Gardner's theory of multiple intelligence lists seven abilities or thought processes, such as:

1. Logic and Math reasoning - mathematical abilities
2. Verbal and Linguistic - meaning of words and language
3. Visual and Spatial - perceptions of space and architecture
4. Musical - sensitivity to musical sounds
5. Interpersonal - relationships and understanding others
6. Intrapersonal - understanding one's own interests
7. Kinesthetic - body skills or abilities

There are many implications that can come from Gardner's theory. One implication is related to low achievers and dropouts. Very often, student dropouts do not perform well in schools that use traditional teaching

---

[12] Barbara Clark, *Optimizing Learning: The Integrative Education Model in the Classroom,* Columbus, Ohio Merrill, 1986, p. 17.

[13] Ibid., 26.

[14] Joseph F. Callahan, Leonard Clark, Richard Kellough, *Teaching in the Middle and Secondary Schools,* 7th Edition, New Jersey: Merrill "Prentice Hall, 2002, 41.

methods that present information in a linear, logical, and sequential way. IQ tests and some standardized tests mainly measure math and verbal abilities, which are only two of the types of intelligence in Gardner's list of seven. However, Gardner's theory includes five other areas of intelligence that also-impact learning, achievement, and the potential for success.

The debates about the value and role of traditional Intelligence Quotients and ways to measure multiple intelligences will no doubt continue for years in research studies.

Emotional Intelligence

Another way of looking at intelligence has come from the work of Daniel Goleman, who has introduced the concept of emotional intelligence into the debate. Human emotions have always had a tremendous impact on human behavior. But how does emotion impact the teaching-learning process?

Daniel Goleman basically defines emotional intelligence as awareness of feelings and anxieties and ability to effectively handle relationships.

He argues that emotional intelligence may be more important for success in life than IQ. In an article in the *USA Weekend*, September 8-10, 1995, Goleman offered an illustration in which he suggested that valedictorians and students with high SAT scores may not be the most successful in life.

Another interesting comment he made was related to healthy and happy marriages. Goleman said, "And if you want a happy, enduring marriage, your EQ, not your IQ, can make the difference."[15] According to Goleman, people who have emotional intelligence are those who are friendly, able to get along with people, have social poise, and are caring and cooperative. In the article above, Goleman provides a quick inventory, or checklist, to test your EQ.

However, one question that teachers can consider related to Goleman's research is: How do emotions affect student learning? The research below suggests some answers.

---

[15] Ibid., 40.

Affective Behavior

Many contemporary studies are finding that a person's affective or emotional behaviors are having an impact on learning achievement, similar to cognitive abilities. Several conclusions about cognitive and affective behavior relationships are reported in the research of Krathwohl, Bloom, and Masia.[16] The following are some of their statements.

"Cognitive achievement is regarded as fair game for grading purposes... because achievement, competence, productivity... are regarded as public matters."[17]

Also, the reporting of honors, like the National Merit Scholarships, etc., are public matters, but one's beliefs, attitudes toward God, and values are private matters. Therefore, public schools have avoided measuring and reporting on affective behaviors, attitudes, and values. However, "the public-private status of cognitive vs. affective behaviors is deeply rooted in the Judeo-Christian religion."[18] But another reason that public schools have stayed away from measuring affective behaviors is the belief that affective behavior, such as attitudes and values, develops slowly, while cognitive behavior, such as knowledge, develops quickly. However, this is not supported by the research of these authors, who say that "it is even possible that just the opposite may be true; namely, that affective behaviors undergo far more sudden transformations than do cognitive behaviors."[19] For a long time, it was also assumed that if a student learned information at the simple knowledge level, this would lead to developing higher cognitive skills of problem solving and analysis. This belief in "automatic" development of higher mental processes is no longer widely held.[20] It was also assumed that

---

[16] Daniel Goleman, "Emotional Intelligences," *USA Weekend*, September, 8-10, 1995, 16.

[17] D.R. Krathwohl, B. Bloom, B. Masia, *Taxonomy of Educational Objectives*, N.Y: David McKay, Inc. 1964, 18.

[18] Ibid., 18.

[19] Ibid., 18.

[20] Ibid., 19.

when there was cognitive achievement, there would also be a corresponding development of positive affective behavioral learning.

But under some conditions, the development of cognitive behaviors (knowledge) may actually destroy affective (emotional or attitudinal) behaviors, and instead of positive cognitive growth, a negative relationship may develop.[21] According to Krathwohl and others, these findings certainly suggest that a student's cognitive learning and affective attitudes and emotions should be given equal attention in and out of the classroom because they have positive and/or negative influences on learning.

The positions that perceptual psychologists have taken regarding affective behavior, is that all behavior is affectively related: "If behavior is a function of personal meanings, then perceptions must become the center of the teaching-learning situation."[22] If the above researchers are correct, then pushing students academically without addressing affective behaviors may have unwanted negative effects on learning.

---

[21] Ibid., 20.

[22] Ibid., 20.

Chapter 8:

Learning Styles

Understanding learning styles is another way for teachers to improve the teaching-learning process. According to Bernice McCarthy, an authority on learning styles, "Style is real and it makes a difference."[23] I believe she is right. However, the primary authority on the uniqueness of human learning styles is God's revelation that declares the uniqueness of His creation of man as His Image. It is because of this uniqueness and diversity that teachers are required to use a variety of methods of instruction. Why? Because God makes all of His children uniquely, created in His image, unique in intellect, appearance, and in spiritual gifts.

This truth is revealed in student learning styles, and teachers need to understand how style impacts learning. But, in a similar way, the teachers own style of learning can impact their teaching methods. "When teachers understand students' learning styles and adjust their teaching to those styles, students will learn."[24] And, when students understand their own styles, they will find that subjects will become meaningful, and they may stop being afraid of certain subjects.[25]

Teachers need to be careful about prejudging some kids as being smart and some as being dumb. It is true that people have intellectual differences,

---

[23] Combs, op. cit. 68.

[24] Marlene D. Le Fever, *Learning Styles: Reaching Everyone God Gave You to Teach*, Cook Communications Ministries, 1995, 5.

[25] Ibid., 11.

but teachers need to be able to adapt their teaching strategies to fit different student learning styles. You can't keep using one method, no matter how effective, to teach all the different kids in the classroom. The following books written by Christian authors are filled with many ideas for parents, teachers, and educational leaders: *Learning Styles: Reaching Everyone God Gave You to Teach*, by Marlene Le Fever and *The Way They Learn* by Cynthia Ulrich Tobias. Many of the ideas below are drawn from these books and other resources.

Le Fever's book: Learning Styles

"A learning style is the way in which a person sees or perceives things best and then processes or uses what has been seen."[26]

Le Fever's book is an excellent resource that offers Christian teachers with numerous ideas and examples to understand and implement learning ideas from the contemporary research model developed by Bernice McCarthy, called the 4MAT System,[27] which describes four kinds of learners:

1. <u>Imaginative Learners.</u> They are listeners, questioners, and like to develop relationships with others.
2. <u>Analytic Learners.</u> They listen carefully for information and data, want answers, and they like the traditional teaching methods.
3. <u>Common Sense Learners.</u> The hands-on type, they want to be doing and applying what they are learning.
4. <u>Dynamic Learners.</u> These are the action types, flexible, and like to follow hunches and take risks.

These four terms define student styles and how each style suggests a different way of learning. Students who exhibit these styles tend to ask themselves four kinds of questions 1) Imaginative learners ask the question, "Why

---

[26] Ibid., 12.
[27] Ibid., 17.

do I need this?" 2) Analytic learners ask, "What does this mean to me?" 3) Common sense learners ask, "How does this work?" and 4) Dynamic learners ask, "How will I use what I've learned?"[28]

Le Fever's book provides a quick checklist on page twenty-nine as a way to determine your dominant style. The checklist is called, "What's My Learning Style?" It is a simple way to help students see if they tend to be like one or more of the four styles listed.

The Way They Learn

Cynthia Tobias's book *The Way They Learn* presents a discussion of several models for understanding how students learn. She explains the following models:

1) Howard Gardner's Multiple Intelligences Theory
2) Witkin's model on processing information analytically or globally.
3) Barbe & Swassing's model on modalities
4) Dunn & Dunn's model on the effects of environment
5) Anthony F. Gregoric's model on how we perceive information

Since Gardner's theory of multiple intelligences has been previously mentioned, the following information will deal with student perception, the classroom environment, how students process information, and how different modalities influence learning.

Before discussing "perception," it should be noted that the following authors, Cynthia Tobias and Marlene Le Fever, are presenting their ideas of perception and learning from a biblical Christian point of view. They are not making the same assumptions about human nature as those made by the "third force" perceptual psychologists Abraham Maslow and Arthur Combs, who were discussed in Part Two of this book. As you recall, they defined human nature from a non-biblical perspective, which does not

---

[28] Ibid., 20.

recognize man as having an inborn sin nature or being created in God's image and likeness.

Cynthia Tobias's book focuses on the importance of recognizing how different learning styles affect learning. According to Tobias, "The way in which we view the world is called 'perception.' Perceptions shape what we think, how we make decisions, and how we define what's important to us. Our individual perceptions also determine our natural learning strengths or learning styles."[29] Tobias's book focuses heavily on the Gregoric model of perception.[30] It's easy to see that Le Fever, McCarthy, and others have defined learning styles in similar ways.

For example, Anthony Gregoric defines perception as the way we view the world around us. And the way we utilize information we perceive, he refers to as our way of organizing or ordering information.

Gregoric says that we perceive information in two ways: 1) **concretely** and 2) **abstractly**. The mind perceives **concretely** through the five senses: sight, touch, smell, feel, and taste. And the mind also perceives **abstractly** by visualizing, and/or believing ideas that we can't actually see. Thus, when we are thinking abstractly, we use our intellect, intuition, imagination, and belief.[31] A person's faith is another example of abstract perception.

Gregoric says that we organize information and we perceive information in two ways: 1) **sequentially**, and 2) **randomly**. **Sequential** organization of information is a step-by-step, or linear, process. For example, some students arrange or organize information from simple to complex. But **randomly** organizing information means that a person can perceive things in large parts or see things as a whole picture or concept.

The Gregoric model identifies four combinations that result from the way a person's mind perceives and organizes information. These combinations are:

---

[29] Ibid., 16.

[30] Cynthia Ulrich Tobias, *The Way They Learn*, Colorado Springs: Focus on the Family, 1994, 14.

[31] Ibid., 14.

Learning Styles

1. Concrete Sequential (CS)
2. Abstract Sequential (AS)
3. Abstract Random (AR)
4. Concrete Random (CR)

According to Gregoric, a person may have one or more of the four styles but will usually have one dominated style. A teacher would do well to examine the Gregoric model to see how it can help in understanding learning styles. Some teachers may even want to examine Gregoric's sophisticated inventory for determining a person's dominant style. However, a very simple checklist, called Dominant Learning Style characteristics, is included in Tobias's book on page twenty-one. Tobias's book gives several helpful examples that describe individuals and/or students who may have one or more of these dominant styles.

Environment

Kenneth and Rita Dunn developed a model that focuses on things within the learning environment, such as the effects of lighting in the classroom, temperature, space used for instruction, time on task, or certain times during the day.

According to Rita Dunn, a few students cannot learn unless a particular element is present or absent.[32] For example, noise is helpful for some, while others prefer a quiet environment. Some students prefer a cool room temperature, and others prefer a warm room. These sound obvious, but they are often overlooked by some teachers who "just want to teach the material"!

Processing Information

The model developed by Herman Witkin explains that there are at least two ways we process and understand information. For example, some people

---

[32] Ibid., 17.

see things as a whole picture, which Witkin calls "global understanding." Other people are able to break things down into smaller parts of the whole picture, which he calls "analytic understanding." Here again, perception is involved in ways of learning. A checklist inventory of these two styles is also included in Tobias's book on page 107.

Modalities

There is nothing easy about teaching and trying to understand all the factors that affect student learning. Walter Barbe and Raymond Swassing developed a model that focuses on a person's modalities, or how we remember information.[33] Barbe and Swassing's model adds another dimension to the complex issue of how we learn.

There are four terms, or learning styles, that educators refer to as "student modalities," which are described as our auditory, visual, kinesthetic, and tactile modalities. An auditory modality refers to the student who learns best by listening through lecture or through teacher talk.

A student who learns more easily by seeing things has a visual modality.

A kinesthetic modality refers to the student who learns by doing or being involved in a hands-on activity. The tactile modality identifies the type of student who learns by physically touching and feeling things. Tobias provides a modality checklist on page ninety in her book.

Summary

All of the models above are explained in Tobias's book, but the summary point is simply this: "Learning styles" have many dimensions. Christian educators attribute these differences to God's creation of every unique individual person. It is evident that people are different in terms of their size, shape, race, color, appearance, intellect, etc. Uniqueness comes from God's amazing design of humans so that no two are exactly alike.

---

[33] Ibid., 77.

Therefore, teachers need to be reminded that every individual is "wonderfully made" with unbelievable differences. When the teacher steps into the classroom to begin instruction, it is the teacher who sets the environment, controls the curriculum, selects the methods, and determines the interaction that will take place. Students come with their unique styles and abilities. "When students are taught in ways that complement their styles, leaders will see significant increased achievement, improved attitudes, and fewer behavior problems."[34]

I have come to believe that the real art and skill of teaching can be discovered by observing the kind of verbal and, possibly, nonverbal interactions between the teacher and students in the classroom.

One final point about learning research needs to be stated. I have omitted the large body of research on learning theory conducted by Madeline Hunter and others because their contributions are so comprehensive and their work includes far more information than this primer can examine.

---

[34] Ibid., 87.

Chapter 9:

Teacher Effectiveness

For many years, there have been numerous studies that have tried to analyze "good teaching." A few of these have been to study and/or examine 1) teacher character traits, 2) teacher activities in the classroom, 3) teacher methods, 4) teacher goals and objectives, 5) student performance (scores), 6) classroom climate, and 7) teacher interaction patterns.

The previous discussions have suggested various ways to help teachers become more effective in trying to improve student learning and achievement. Other suggestions for improving teacher effectiveness have been to 1) make courses more difficult, 2) increase homework, 3) improve discipline, 4) improve student achievement, 5) improve teacher training, and 6) provide more money for education. While all of these suggestions have merit, the focus of this final section will be on teacher-student interaction and classroom climate.

Teacher-Student Interaction

Social forces in the classroom are complex, but the verbal behavior between the teacher and student is a significant indicator of teaching patterns (styles) that teachers exhibit and the student responses to the patterns of teaching. And a few of these ideas and findings have come from a body of research, using a system called "Interaction Analysis."

One of the research findings indicates that it is the teacher's talk or verbal behavior that mainly determines positive or negative interaction. This point has been documented by many studies, and some of these studies are mentioned below.

During the past five decades, a large body of research on teacher effectiveness and teacher-student interactions in the classroom has been conducted and analyzed by J.P. Anderson, A. Bellack, M.L. Cogan, E.J. Amidon, and N.A. Flanders, and others. I will discuss only the work of Amidon and Flanders, who have conducted many studies that focus on teacher and student interaction in the classroom. A few of the ideas and findings have come from the body of research using a system called "Interaction Analysis." The system and findings are briefly reported below.

"Interaction analysis" is a ten-category observation system developed primarily as a tool to be used by the classroom teacher, a colleague, or an outside observer who is trained to use and analyze teacher and student interactions in the classroom during the presentation of a lesson. The assumption that Amidon, et.al., made in developing their observation system is that verbal behavior is an adequate sample of one's total behavior.[35] This seemed to be a reasonable assumption because many observations revealed that teachers tend to do most of the talking during their teaching in the classroom.

Amadon, et. al., developed a ten-category system to analyze teachers' verbal statements and student responses to those statements. The ten categories are divided into three parts. Part one is a list of seven teacher talking behaviors (comments). Part two lists two types of student responses to the teacher's talk (behavior). And part three observes the amount of silence, noise, or the kind of general confusion going on during the lesson. The categories are carefully defined in the materials produced by Amadon, et. al., but will not be defined here. A brief list of the ten categories is presented below to show the kinds of "talk" from the teacher and students.

---

[35] E. J. Amidon and N.A. Flanders, *"The Role of the Teacher in the Classroom: Interaction Analysis for Teachers,* Revised Third Edition, St. Paul, MN,: Amidon & Associates, 1985, 4.

Interaction Analysis Categories

<u>Seven categories that describes the type of teacher talk</u>

1. Accepting students' feelings
2. Praising students
3. Using student ideas
4. Asking students
5. Lecturing
6. Giving directions
7. Criticizing a student

<u>Two categories of student talk or responses to the teacher</u>

8. Responding to direct questions or comments
9. Student initiating a question or idea

<u>Category Ten</u>:

10. Classroom silence or confusion

In part one of the ten category system, numbers one, two, and three of teacher talk are analyzed as being indirect (or encouraging) teacher comments. Teacher behaviors (comments) four through seven are analyzed as direct teacher comments and/or influence on students. As you might realize, some of these teacher comments can be positive or negative, helpful or discouraging. And, of course, in all seven categories of teacher talk, it is the teacher who is "normally" in control and deliberately or inadvertently chooses which kind of teacher influence to use.[36]

The system is designed to systematically observe, record, and analyze three parts of the interaction, which will produce numerical tallies and a

---

[36] Ibid.

pattern of teacher-student interaction that is put in a visual matrix for the teacher to see. The whole system is explained in books and materials that present interaction analysis. One recommended book and manual is in the bibliography.

The primary purpose of the system is for teacher self-appraisal, and it's one way to help teachers see how they might improve their teaching patterns. With training, the individual teacher can begin to analyze one aspect of their effectiveness and interaction patterns. Below are just a few of the findings relevant to teaching and learning that have resulted from research that used this system of interaction analysis.

Findings From Interaction Analysis Research

One of the more interesting findings indicated that during a typical teaching lesson in most classrooms, teachers talk about 70 percent of the time, and students talk (respond) about 20 percent of the time during the teaching lesson. This pattern is consistently true in most secondary classes and in most subjects. It is less true at the elementary level.

However, a significant point seems to indicate that many teachers assume that they are supposed to do most of the talking and information giving, and students are to listen and absorb the information. This body of research concludes that teacher talk or lecture was the primary teaching method in most classes where these studies and percentages were recorded.

With this kind of result, many teachers must have assumed that student learning is best accomplished through student listening. My experience indicates that many teachers who I have observed over the years still believe they should do most of the talking in the classroom. However, this assumption has been challenged as being invalid by many studies, and probably many classroom teachers would agree.

While some students learn through listening, others are turned off. Also, this teaching method or approach extremely limits students who learn through many different learning styles and modalities, as previously discussed.

Another interesting finding (observation) is related to the 70 percent of teacher talk, 20 percent of student talk, and 10 percent of silence or confusion. This finding indicated that the interactions were mostly "direct patterns" (teacher dominated), rather than "indirect patterns" (student initiated). Indirect patterns allow students more opportunity to discuss, debate, and/or give their ideas about the lesson. When the teacher talk volume was at the 70 percent level, most of it was lecturing and asking questions, which required student recall from memory, a response to teacher direction, or responding to questions that called for right or wrong answers. This is often a kind of drill pattern.

Another important finding was that the first three categories of teacher talk were seldom used in most classes, while categories four and five were heavily used. Using categories one, two, and three identifies an "indirect" teaching method, which encourages more student interaction, involvement, and discussion. Using categories four and five generally reflects a teacher's "direct" teaching method of instruction, which is certainly appropriate for some lessons, but it also allows less time and fewer opportunities for students to discuss, express opinions, ask questions for clarification, and interact with other students. Thus, a heavy percentage (70 percent) of teacher talk, which emphasized lecture and questioning, greatly limited the time (20 percent) for student talk and interaction.

Recent studies on cooperative learning indicates that allowing students opportunity to discuss and interact with other students and the teacher can be a valuable method for involving students in their own learning process. Below are some brief findings from the research of Amidon and Flanders utilizing the system of interaction analysis in the classroom.

Some Implications from IA Research

1. When teacher's talk is 70 percent of the class time, there is little time for student talk, and this can sometimes have a negative effect on learning.

Teaching Is Interaction

2. Praising and using student ideas and allowing time for student talk improves student attitudes, achievement, and behavior.
3. Effective teachers use a variety of interaction patterns, styles, and methods.
4. Effective teachers talk less and encourage students to initiate talk. (This is usually accomplished by using categories one, two, and three.)

An Observation Instrument for Classroom Climate

Concerned teachers have always been sensitive to student attitudes in the classroom. Another researcher, Bruce Tuckman, after years of teaching developed an observation instrument designed to evaluate classroom climate.[37]

He defined "classroom climate" as the overall attitude that teachers and students have toward each other. It's the tone in the classroom, and it grows out of the interaction between the teacher and the students, as well as interactions among other students.

According to Tuckman, once a positive climate is established, it 1) fosters helpful interactions among students, 2) improves the experiences and respect between the teacher and students, 3) gives momentum to classroom activities, and 4) improves learning. One of the main conclusions from his research, and that of others, was the recognition that the teacher sets the climate in the classroom.[38]

By the end of his career and research, he arrived at the following conclusion:

It is possible to sum up all the research on classroom climate in one sentence and it can easily serve as the overall reason for positive climate: Education conducted in an atmosphere which is positive is desirable--teachers

---

[37] 46, Ibid.

[38] Bruce Tuckman, *"How to Observe and Improve Classroom Climate,"* Evaluating Instructional Programs, 1985, 30, (LB2823, T93).

teach better, students learn more, and attitudes toward schools improves as climate moves from negative to positive.[39]

Professor Bruce Tuckman of Rutgers University published a simple but valid and reliable instrument for assessing classroom climate. This instrument is to be used to observe classroom climate and help the teacher gather feedback concerning climate.

A Biblical Analogy

I would like to close Part Three with a biblical analogy which I have adapted from an article by A. Ribero Netto,[40] who used the Parable of the Sower from the gospel of Mathew 13:3-8. The passage of the Sower seems to me to illustrate a type of relationship between farming and education. However, I am not suggesting that the analogy that I am making is a valid interpretation of this scripture. But I would like to make the point that I personally see a kind of comparison or relationship between a "farmer," who sows seeds in the ground on his farm, and a "teacher," who sows seeds of knowledge and moral values in a school classroom.

The farmer sows "good seed" in good soil, but he will also have to depend on good climate conditions to produce an abundant crop at harvest time. Of course, the farmer will also have to cultivate and care for the seedlings as they grow to maturity. The farmer knows that there many variables, such as bugs, insects, and bad weather, that can hinder a productive harvest time.

In a similar way, the teacher in the classroom daily cultivates students who are like young tender seedlings. It is the role of the teacher to set the climate so the young seedlings can grow in knowledge and in their relationship with their teacher, fellow students, and their commitment to God.

---

[39] Ibid.

[40] Ibid.
    A. Ribeiro Netto, "Seed, Soil and Climate: What a Minimum Harvest is and How to Assess It,"
    B. *Studies in Educational Evaluation*, Vol 11, 1985, pp. 245-247.

Teaching Is Interaction

In this analogy, the students (seeds) need the care and nourishment that comes from a positive climate and environment of love and encouragement that is established by the classroom teacher. It is the teacher who controls the interaction patterns that play a critical role in the kind of effective teaching that will produce an abundant harvest at graduation from their Christian school.

Although parents, teachers, and a Christian education are very important, the real source of abundant growth comes from the study of God's Word, leading from the Holy Spirit of Truth, and the student's commitment to the authority of Jesus Christ.

Summary

If the teacher recognizes the unique differences of students and sets a positive climate that encourages relationships with the teacher and other students, the result will be academic achievement, good moral behavior, and righteousness toward God.

Classroom climate, teacher-student interaction, learning styles, intelligence, religious values, teacher methods, and other variables are all connected to teacher effectiveness and student learning.

A Christian school's ability to produce students who will grow spiritually and academically is directly related to all teachers and Christian educators. Parents have the primary responsibility to support a Christian education for their children. This is an impossible task unless Christians pray for the Lord's help.

Children are a heritage from the Lord, and unless the Lord builds your house and a Christian school, all the labor is in vain (Ps. 127:1-3).

Part Four:
Ideas for Evaluation

Introduction

Monitoring education data collected provides valuable feedback for parents, teachers, administrators, and the governing board. Systematic evaluation of an educational program is an important part of determining effectiveness. The term "evaluation" usually implies a comprehensive activity of data collection and analysis of an educational program. The term "assessment" usually refers to various types of student achievement and/or performance on tests. A systematic approach to evaluation of an education program must develop ways to deal with both evaluation and assessment.

An education program must first identify the overall purpose and mission for education. There are many ways and areas to be systematically evaluated in order to determine the school's effectiveness.

For example, the following areas have had a significant impact on educational outcomes:

1) The organizational structure of a school
2) Facilities and equipment
3) Costs and financial support
4) Administrative services
5) Qualifications and skills of teachers
6) An appropriate curriculum
7) Parent involvement
8) Counseling services
9) Community support

Other factors could be listed, but you can see that evaluation is a comprehensive task, and the above areas all play a vital role in the educational process. Systematic evaluation is a means for providing feedback to parents, teachers, and the school board about the overall academic and affective goals.

Instructional Evaluation

Evaluation of the instructional program has the specific purpose of providing feedback for students, teachers, and administrators for improving instructional strategies, student achievement, and meeting the spiritual needs that are essential to the purpose of public, private, or Christian education programs.

One model used by J.P. Guilford at the University of California in the 1960s to identify a theoretical structure of the intellect. And in the 1970s, a similar cube-like model was developed at the University of Arizona by Dr. Robert Hammond to identify variables for evaluating public school programs. The Arizona model gives examples of the many possible combinations that can be identified for instructional evaluation.

Description Of Variables

The models or paradigms above describe three dimensions to consider when evaluating student learning outcomes. 1) Student cognitive, affective, and physical behaviors, 2) Instructional variables such as content, teaching methods, and facilities, and 3) people variables, such as teacher skills, administrators, parents, and others who influence education.

The above examples in figures one and two point out the numerous combinations of variables that impact instructional learning outcomes in a positive or negative way.

Paradigms & Models

Implementing a paradigm such as this or any other model is a difficult task. But this kind of approach, discussed in the introduction represents only one way to organize and gather continuous data that may lead toward developing a quality educational program. A paradigm is not a panacea to bring about a quality educational program, but it may offer some helpful ideas for improving an educational program.

Quality teachers, administrators, supportive parents, and board leadership are the best hope for excellence. Paradigms and models present only ideas and examples of systematic and continuous evaluation.

Biibliography

1. Amidon, E. J. and Flanders, N. A. <u>The Role of the teacher in the Classroom: Interaction Analysis for Teachers</u>. Revised 3rd Edition. St. Paul, MN: Amidon & Associates. 1985.

2. Association for Supervision and Curriculum Development. <u>Perceiving, Behaving, Becoming: A New Focus for Education</u>. Washington, D. C.: NEA, 1962.

3. Barna, George. <u>A Fish Out of Water</u>. Nashville, TN: Integrity Publishers. 2000.

4. Barton, David. <u>Four Centuries of American Education</u>. Aledo, TX: WallBuilders Press. 2004.

5. Bigge, Morris L. <u>Learning Theories for Teachers</u>. N. Y.: Harper & Row. 1964.

6. Birdsall, Eugene H. "How to Implement the Christian Philosophy," <u>The Philosophy of Christian School Education</u>. Editor, Paul A. Kienel. Association of Christian Schools International. 1978.

7. Bloom, Benjamin S. <u>Taxonomy of Educational Objectives</u>. N. Y.: David McKay, Inc. 1956.

8 . Braley, James W. "The Christian Philosophy Applied to methods of Instruction." <u>The Philosophy of Christian School Education</u>. Editor, Paul A. Kienel. Association of Christian Schools International. 1978.

9. Callahan, Joseph F., Leonard Clark, Richard Kellough. <u>Teaching in the Middle and Secondary Schools</u>. 7th Edition. New Jersey: Merrill Prentice Hall. 2002.

10. Clark, Barbara. Optimizing Learning: The Integrative Education Model in the Classroom. Columbus, Ohio: Merrill. 1986.

11. Combs, A. W. Myths in Education. Boston: Allyn & Bacon, Inc. 1979.

12. Delk, David. "Theology for Ordinary Life," By Faith. Published by the Presbyterian Church in America. May-June, 2005.

13. Dobson, James. The New Dare to Discipline. Wheaton: Tyndale. 1992.

14. Garrick, Gene. "Developing Educational Objectives," The Philosophy of Christian School Education. Editor, Paul A. Kienel. Association of Christian Schools International. 1978.

15. ibbs, David C. and Jerry Newcombe. One nation Under God. Florida: Christian Law Association. 2005.

16. Hocking, David L. "The Theological Basis for the Philosophy of Christian School Education," The Philosohphy of Christian School Education. Editor, Paul, A. Kienel. ACSI. 1978.

17. Kienel, Paul A. The Christian School: Why It Is Right for your Child. Victor Books. 1974.

18. Kienel, Paul A. Editor. The Philosophy of Christian School Education. Association of Christian Schools International. 1978.

19. Kienel, Paul A. Reasons for Christian Schools. Mott Media. 1981.

20. Krathwohl, D.R., B, Bloom, B. Masia. Taxonomy of Educational Objectives. N.Y.,: David McKay, Inc. 1964.

21. Land, Richard and John Perry, Real Homeland Security: How Godly Families Protect a Nation. Colorado: Alive communications, Inc. 2003.

22. Le Fever, Marlene D. Learning Styles: Reaching Everyone God Gave You To Teach. Cook Communications Ministries. 1995.

23. Lowrie, Roy W. Jr. Serving God on the Christian School Board. Western Association of Christian Schools and National Christian School Education Association. 1976.

24. Morris, Henry M. Education for the Real World. Creation Life Publishers. 1977.

25. Netto, A. Ribeiro. "Seed, Soil and Climate: What a Minimum Harvest Is and How to Assess It.," Studies in Educational Evaluation. Vol. 11, pp. 245-247, 1985.

26. Perrin, Christopher A. An Introduction to Classical Education: A Guide for Parents. Harrisburg, PA: Classical Academic Press. 2004.

27. Tackett, Del. "The Truth Project." Focus on the Family, Copyright, 2006.

28. Tobias, Cynthia Ulrich. The Way They Learn. Colorado Springs: Focus on the Family. 1994.

29. Wilson, Douglas. The Case for Classical Christian Education. Wheaton, Il: Crossway Books. 2003.

www.ingramcontent.com/pod-product-compliance
Ingram Content Group UK Ltd.
Pitfield, Milton Keynes, MK11 3LW, UK
UKHW042004230426
12048UKWH00009B/541